CW00855038

A Newbies Guide to LinkedIn

Tips, Tricks and Insider Hints for Using LinkedIn

Minute Help Guides

Minute Help Press
www.minutehelp.com

© 2012. All Rights Reserved.

Table of Contents

Chapter 1: What is LinkedIn?

LinkedIn is a professional social network with over 120 million members. This network allows users to stay in touch with colleagues, employers and friends while establishing and controlling a professional profile. Unlike Facebook, which has a broad social reach, LinkedIn is a professionally-focused network. There are no check-ins at local bars, photos of children's friends, or walls to post comments. Instead, LinkedIn is dedicated to building business connections, making new contacts, job searching and recruitment, and finding expert ideas and answers.

LinkedIn users may join the site for free and create a personal profile. The profile consists of a profile photo (optional), current and past employment, education, recommendations, and optional links to a personal website or Twitter. Users create a brief summary of their professional work experience and accomplishments, and may also list professional specialties, such as "legal marketing", "crisis communication", "writing" or "government relations." Finally, users list reasons why they can be contacted, ranging from "career opportunities" and "expertise requests" to "getting back in touch" and "business deals."

Find and Be Found

The purpose of LinkedIn is to connect with as many professionals as possible. The primary reason to join LinkedIn is simple: find and be found. Unlike Facebook or Twitter, there's no exclusivity or desire to maintain a small, trusted circle of friends for information sharing. With LinkedIn, the more connections you have, then the wider your overall reach.

Your network is loosely defined as your direct connections, your second-degree connections (individuals directly connected with your connections), and your third degree connections (the second-degree connections of your connections. For example, an individual with only 33 direct connections could be "linked in" to over one million people thanks to second and third-degree connections. A network that's over one million strong is a powerful professional resource. LinkedIn adds one member every second, which means that your network is constantly growing. Even if you are not actively making new contacts, there's a good chance that your contacts are. In the image below, you'll see that the user's network grew by 3,061 people in just a few days – thanks to adding a few direct contacts that indirectly added thousands more.

Your LinkedIn Network

33 Connections link you to 1,029,711+ professionals

3,061 New people in your Network since April 9

LinkedIn's "linking" system means that when you perform a search for individuals in a specific industry with specific skills, you'll end up with hundreds of results – even if your network is only a handful of people. In the example above, the user has just 33 direct connections. But thanks to secondary and tertiary connections, the user's network is over one million strong. This means that any search performed will query the user profiles of over one million people.

So just how important is LinkedIn for business professionals? When it comes to professional networking on social media sites, LinkedIn wins hands-down. Researchers at Lab42, a market research firm, found that 61% of social media users choose LinkedIn for their professional networking, with over one-third of users checking the site daily, and over two-thirds of users checking the site at least several times per week.

Free vs. Paid Membership – Which is right for you?

LinkedIn offers two levels of membership: free (basic) accounts and paid accounts. The vast majority of users have free accounts.

There are three types of paid individual accounts:
- **Business** ($24.95/mo) – Includes three InMails per month, 300 profiles per search and five folders in the Profile Organizer
- **Business Plus** ($49.95/mo) – Includes 10 InMails per month, 500 profiles per search and 25 folders in the Profile Organizer
- **Pro** ($99.95/mo) – Includes 50 InMails per month, 700 profiles per search and 25 folders in the Profile Organizer.

All paid accounts include access to specifics on who has recently viewed your profile, the ability to enable "OpenLink" messaging so anyone (with or without a connection) can contact you, name access to third-degree and group connections, and expanded profile views of everyone on LinkedIn (even if you are not currently connected).

Should you upgrade to a paid account? Probably not. Even if you are looking for a job, most people find jobs based off referrals, group memberships or the "Jobs You May Be Interested In" job postings (currently in beta). LinkedIn does offer special account opportunities for job seekers. We'll discuss these account plans in greater detail under "Finding Jobs".

LinkedIn paid accounts are geared primarily towards headhunters, recruiters and HR representatives. These individuals rely heavily on in-depth people searches and InMail to discover and vet potential job candidates. LinkedIn also offers special paid accounts for recruiters (such as the Talent Pro account for $499.95/mo) and sales professionals (such as the Sales Executive Account for $99.95/mo). The majority of users, however, will receive the plenty of benefits from the regular unpaid account.

Chapter 2: Five Key Reasons Why People Use LinkedIn

LinkedIn is more than just a network of professional business contacts. With nearly two-thirds of users logging on several times a week, LinkedIn is an active, dynamic network of professionals exchanging information, crowdsourcing business problems to industry experts, building and maintaining professional contacts, promoting businesses, and finding new jobs or work.

LinkedIn offers great flexibility in how the networking service can be used. According to Lab42, top-level executives primarily use it for industry networking and promoting their business. Middle management uses LinkedIn for keeping in touch with coworkers, coworker networking and industry networking. Entry-level employees use LinkedIn primarily for job searching, co-worker networking and keeping in touch with coworkers.

Over 90% of LinkedIn users rate the site as "professionally useful". Users told Lab42 that LinkedIn helps them "connect to individuals in my industry as possible clients", "is more professional than Facebook" and "allows me to hire people I wouldn't regularly meet."

Five Key Reasons Why People Join LinkedIn

1. **Getting back in touch.** LinkedIn is based on the principle that users want to find others and be found themselves. This is very different from other social sites, like Facebook, where many members add layers of privacy to keep personal photos, profiles and interests private. Because of LinkedIn's advanced search functionality and contact importer, LinkedIn makes finding contacts easy. Most importantly, your contacts want to be found. That's the whole reason that they are on LinkedIn. Lost touch with an old coworker or classmate? If you both list the same employee or school in your profile, you can find each other and reconnect in less than five minutes.

2. **Career management insurance.** Let's face it: between work and family commitments, the thought of attending networking happy hours and lunching with former coworkers just to "stay in touch" can be exhausting. There are simply not enough hours in the day to regularly network. Unfortunately, neglecting to network can lead to serious problems down the road if you lose your job or need to change jobs quickly. If you haven't stayed in touch,

tracking down a former boss or coworker for advice or a recommendation can be a hassle. Save yourself the stress and anxiety of urgent, last-minute networking by maintaining your network all along. Think of LinkedIn as "free career management insurance" – it's there when you need it. LinkedIn is an easy place to reconnect with colleagues and connect with individuals who share your career interests. When it comes time to start the job search, you've got a ready-made network to tap into for information interviews. It's that easy.

3. **Acquiring and sharing expertise.** With nearly one million groups on LinkedIn, there's a professional group for everyone. Groups are the perfect place to network with power figures in your industry. Have a question? Post it to your group for expert feedback and analysis. Check your group's "Top Influencers" board to connect with the most influential members. Search and discover interesting discussions that broaden your knowledge. Make yourself more valuable to your current employer by increasing your expertise.

4. **Searching for new jobs or work.** When it comes to the job search, LinkedIn is ground zero for many job searchers. Search for companies that are hiring in your field of expertise. Discover contacts with a connection to your dream company. Leverage these

connections for an information interview. In addition to searching for a new job, many professionals use LinkedIn to find new work opportunities. For example, freelance technical writers can network with contacts to learn about new project assignments.

5. **Hiring new employees.** Post a job, search for new candidates and build your business's brand on your company page. LinkedIn's paid recruiting membership services place powerful talent search filters at your fingertips, and even automate the search process – sending you daily updates with candidates that match your specific search requirements.

Chapter 3: Should You Use LinkedIn?

You've heard a lot about how great LinkedIn is. But does that mean it's right for you? In a word: yes. No matter where you are in your career, LinkedIn is a valuable professional network. Whether you need to change jobs, expand your business contacts, or stay in touch with old colleagues while you work part-time or take time off, LinkedIn will keep you in the loop. In fact, if you are not using LinkedIn, you're missing out on job and networking opportunities.

Many people choose not to join Twitter or Facebook, objecting to a constant stream of social notifications, wedding and baby photos, and inane status updates. Sure, reading that Joe (an old high school classmate with whom you haven't spoken to in 15 years) is upset that his March Madness bracket went bust adds little value to your life. But what if Joe knew about a job opportunity in your field? What if Joe lives in the same city where you are relocating and could serve as an introduction to new colleagues? If you were connected with Joe on LinkedIn, then you could enjoy these professional benefits without hearing about his March Madness bracket.

Increasingly, businesses use LinkedIn to recruit new talent and reach out to potential job candidates. Consider these statistics:

- More than 120 million business professionals use LinkedIn.
- In 2011, 7,610 searches were performed on LinkedIn every 60 seconds.
- From 2010 to 2011, the number of global users visiting LinkedIn every month more than doubled, from 45.8 million in September 2010 to 94.3 million in September 2011. (Quantcast)
- LinkedIn is a network for established professionals: In 2011, 38% of users are 35-49, 32% are aged 50 and over, and just 26% are 18-34. (Quantcast)
- LinkedIn users are affluent professionals: 39% of users have a household income over six-figures; 29% have an income between $60,000 and $100,000.

Ready to get started? Read on for tips to quickly build your profile and jump-start your network.

Chapter 4: The Basics

Setting Up Your Profile

To get started, go to http://linkedin.com. To register, you'll need to enter your email, name and password. LinkedIn will guide you through the steps of adding basic information to your profile. You may also upload a resume, which LinkedIn will use to simplify the process of adding basic education and professional information to your profile.

When getting started, it's important that you enter all your professional and academic experience. You don't need to be detailed – you can always come back later and add specifics. However, adding the companies where you've worked and the schools that you've attended will help you locate contacts and quickly build your network. When entering the name of a business, for example, you'll notice that LinkedIn will attempt to auto-fill your profile with linked-to already established companies. If your company comes up, be sure to select it. This makes it easier to link up with present and former co-workers. The same goes for college and graduate programs – select the correct school on the list with detailed information (e.g., University of Pennsylvania – Wharton) to ensure that you are linked to the correct group.

Navigating LinkedIn

Home Screen

Once you've logged in, you'll see the main profile screen. At the top is a tool bar with links to your profile, contacts, groups, jobs and in-box. Any invitations you receive to connect with other LinkedIn users will appear in your in-box under "invitations". At the top of the Home page is a status update box. Just like on Facebook, you can share an update and also attach a link. You can also link your Twitter account to LinkedIn, so that your tweets will also be shared with your LinkedIn network.

Underneath the status bar is "LinkedIn Today", a collection of headline stories LinkedIn thinks you may be interested in based on your profile and group memberships. If you don't want to see this list when you login, you can hide it by clicking the 'x' button in the right corner.

Underneath "LinkedIn Today" is the "Updates" feed. You can filter updates based on connections, shares, groups, profiles and more. Like Facebook's newsfeed, this tracks recent activity by your contacts and groups. To change your visibility, simply click on a blue link or click the "more" drop down menu for additional options.

On the right column are a list of people you may know (based on your current contacts), ads by LinkedIn members, a link to see who has recently viewed your profile in the last three months, and job openings that you may be interested in based on your professional experience and group affiliations.

Profile

Clicking the "profile" button at the top of the screen takes you straight to your profile. Click the blue "Edit" button next to any of the different profile sections to add or edit your information. Once your initial profile is set up, take a few minutes to fill in details for your professional experience. This is especially important if you have had a non-traditional career trajectory or are trying to break into a new professional field. Only listing companies and your position does not give a full picture of your accomplishments or abilities. Briefly highlight successful projects, initiatives and skills from each job. Now is a great opportunity to succinctly present yourself to potential employees or clients. There's no need to exhaustively list everything – pick the two to three accomplishments that matter most for each job and highlight these.

Contacts

The contacts menu allows you to view and organize current contacts, search for new contacts and view contact suggestions from LinkedIn. If you are just getting started with LinkedIn, consider importing contacts from your email account (such as Google) or importing desktop contacts through Outlook or Apple Mail. To do so, go to Contacts -> Add Connections. You can also view alumni network contacts by selecting your school from the drop down menu underneath "Contacts". From here, you can further filter by dates (such as matching up your dates for attendance and graduation), where alumni work, industry type, and location where they are based. See "Jump-start your network" for detailed information on importing contacts from your email address book.

Inbox

This is a link to your LinkedIn mail inbox. You'll see contact requests as well as messages from different contacts (or those who wish to connect) in this box. To view your invitations, click Inbox -> Invitations. To send a message, either go to Inbox -> Compose (on the left side of the screen) or while viewing any contact, select the "Send Message" option.

Jobs

This link takes you straight to LinkedIn's job search engine, "Jobs for you" (beta). We'll discuss how to search for jobs and post jobs later in this guide.

Companies

Search for companies to follow or see current employees of companies that you have listed in your professional profile.

Five "Must-Do's" for Getting Started

1. **Fill out your *entire* profile – including the headshot.** LinkedIn is one of the top search results that appear on Google. A complete LinkedIn page helps you stand out and concisely supplies information to potential employers, clients and contacts. Chose a current, professional headshot. People like to know with whom they are doing business. This is especially important for individuals who work as independent contractors and freelancers and may never meet the client face-to-face. After you complete your profile, ask a friend to check the spelling and grammar. Your LinkedIn profile is a digital

snapshot of your resume. A spelling or grammar error makes a poor first impression on would-be clients and employers.

2. **Keep your profile up to date.** Job promotion? New work project? Industry award recognition? Regularly update your profile to reflect your current professional accomplishments. Add examples of your work or share industry news. Your profile is a snapshot of you – be sure that individuals can see your recent projects, accomplishments and industry contacts.

3. **Start building connections.** When you first join, LinkedIn will suggest possible contacts based on people you may know. Establishing LinkedIn connections is no time to be exclusive. Think of each contact as a possible job connection. Oftentimes, it's the "weakest" connections (i.e., the people we barely know) that end up bringing us the biggest jobs and clients. Start by importing your email lists. Connect with everyone, even individuals you may not know well. If you are recently married and changed names, consider including your maiden name in your profile. Make it easy for individuals to find and connect with you. Studies show that people prefer to do business with individuals with whom they share a common connection. This builds trust and credibility. The more

LinkedIn contacts, the better.

4. **Join groups within your industry.** Search the "Groups" section on LinkedIn using key terms in your industry. Get started by joining several large groups. This is an easy way to make secondary and tertiary contacts, and it's an easy icebreaker when requesting an introduction. To join a group, select "Groups" from the main menu bar. Initially, selecting a group can seem overwhelming. Start by pursuing groups that LinkedIn suggests may be a good fit based on your profile and interests. To see a list of possible groups, go to Groups -> "Groups You May Like". A lock symbol next to the group means that approval is required for membership. Simply click "Join" and a request for membership will be submitted. Don't see what you need? You can also create your own group.

5. **Showcase your business: add URLS to your profile.** This is your place to shine! Add a link back to your company's website or your personal website portfolio. Instead of just including the URL link, hyperlink text that reads "My Profile", "My Blog" or "My Website". This way, individuals know exactly what they are clicking on. Adding hyperlinks to your LinkedIn profile is an easy way to increase site traffic. Set your view preferences to "full view" so search engines can grab your URL link info as well.

How to Jump-Start Your Network

When you first join LinkedIn, it can seem pretty lonely – especially if you have hundreds of Facebook friends or Twitter followers. Jump-start your network by importing contact lists from Google or Outlook.

For Gmail, Yahoo, Hotmail, AOL and other web-based email programs:
1. From the Contacts dropdown menu at the top of the home page, select "Add Contacts"
2. Enter your email address and password
3. Check the box in front of any contacts with whom you'd like to connect; clicking on the box above the first contact will de-select everyone.

For Outlook, Mac Mail or other desktop based applications, you will first need to create a CSV file. The following instructions for Outlook are also applicable to other desktop-based mail programs:
1. From Outlook, select Import and Export
2. Select "comma separated values (Windows)" and click Next
3. Select the contacts folder for export and click Next
4. Enter a name for your file and click Next
5. Check Export and click Next

NOTE: If your CSV file contains accent marks, you will need to manually remove these marks before uploading the file to LinkedIn.

Upload your file to LinkedIn:
1. From the Contacts dropdown menu, select "Add Connections"
2. Select "Import you desktop email contacts"
3. Select browse and upload your CSV file
4. Check the box in front of any contacts with whom you'd like to connect; clicking on the box above the first contact will de-select everyone.

Chapter 5: Customizing LinkedIn

Your LinkedIn profile is an important part of your public persona and personal brand. In order to get the most out of LinkedIn, you will need to customize your profile, balancing the need for a personalized touch with your public persona. Your profile – above all else – must be professional. Consider this cautionary tale. One LinkedIn user, searching for new ways to promote his small business, decided to embed a video in his LinkedIn profile that automatically played anytime someone visited his page. Instead of selling product samples, the video had the opposite effect, causing him to actually lose connections. Embedding a video may seem like a savvy marketing technique, but it's the equivalent to screaming "BRING ME BUSINESS!" in a potential client's face the very first time you meet them. Yikes – talk about off-putting!

Under "Additional Information", LinkedIn allows users to add hobbies and interests to their public profile. Is this a good idea? Probably not – getting too personal may help you connect with some people, but be a turn off to others. Save the favorite TV shows and weekend hobbies for Facebook. Instead, spend your energy customizing the parts of your profile that matter most.

10 Tips for Customizing Your LinkedIn Profile

1. **Include a professional headshot.** We've already mentioned the importance of including a professional headshot when setting up your profile, but we really can't emphasize this enough. It all comes down to social media credibility. No one likes communicating with a faceless person. Your headshot is your brand. This is not the place for a company logo, family pet photo, or artsy Instagram shot. A professional headshot instantly connotes professionalism and credibility, which is essential to growing your network.

2. **Claim your personal URL.** This is an absolute must, especially if you have a common name. Just like your professional headshot, a custom URL is part of your brand. No one likes being directed to a site via a long chain of random numbers. A custom URL includes your name, such as **www.linkedin.com/in/john.smith**. To create a custom URL, go to Settings -> Edit Your Profile -> Customize Your Public Profile URL. Add your name to the custom box.

3. **Brand your headline.** This is the single most important piece of real estate in your LinkedIn profile. Remember, it's all about building your

personal brand. The space underneath your name is your tagline. When someone searches for you on LinkedIn, this headline will appear next to your name. Anytime you answer a question, your headline will be right there, too. This is your five-second elevator introduction. What do you do? What makes you unique? There are plenty of profiles with "Fortune 500 Account Executive". No one cares about your current job title – this doesn't tell a potential contact anything about your skills or expertise. "Award-winning Writer & New Media Consultant" instantly tells contacts three important things: (1) you're good at what you do (you've won awards!), (2) you have two unique skills (writing and new media), and (3) you provide strategic advice as a consultant.

4. **Brand your summary with keywords.** After your headline, your summary is the second most important part of your LinkedIn profile. This is where you can truly brand yourself and your professional accomplishments. Write a short, compelling professional introduction, just like the executive summary at the top of your resume. Be sure to include keywords relevant to your processional background and expertise, which will improve your ranking in search results. Avoid keyword "stuffing" – which sounds like spam and will have your profile flagged – by naturally including keyword terms where they make sense.

5. **List ALL your schools.** Alumni networks are an ideal way to connect with other LinkedIn users without going to extremes. If someone is in your network, there's no need to request an introduction, join a group or send a paid InMail message. So be sure that ALL your alumni networks are listed, including high school and any study abroad programs. Did you study at King's College in London your junior year of college? Then list that school and the dates you attended.

6. **List ALL your professional experience.** Just like with alumni networks, listing all your companies allows past colleagues to easily find and connect with you. If you have a disjointed or non-traditional professional path (i.e., you started in investment banking, and now you work as a freelance photographer), use your job descriptions to selectively highlight specific accomplishments from each job. You may even wish to address your non-traditional path in your summary. This is an opportunity to highlight the skills you have gained at different jobs and create a compelling narrative that resonates with potential contacts.

7. **Include detailed job descriptions.** This is where you really shine! Use your resume to detail your professional accomplishments and responsibilities at each job. For each position,

list at least one major project that you were responsible for executing. Just like with your resume, quantify your accomplishments. Did your project increase revenues by 30%? Then tell us! Keep your bulleted points brief and to the point. Include keywords for your industry to improve your standing in search results.

8. **List personal websites and social profiles.** LinkedIn allows you to list up to three different websites in your profile. Don't simply default and list your current company's website. Take advantage of this real estate! Do you have a Twitter profile you want to promote? What about a personal website or blog? Including this in your listing is an easy way to increase your followers on other social networks and drive traffic to your website.

9. **Create a profile in a second language.** Even if English is your primary language, in today's globalized economy, a LinkedIn profile in a second language opens you up to a whole new network. This is especially important if your business or network has a high concentration of contacts in a second language (e.g., Chinese) or region (e.g., Latin America). Customize your profile by translating it to a second language. To do so, go to Profile -> Edit Profile -> Create your profile in another language (see link in upper right corner). LinkedIn will automatically translate your profile based on the existing information.

Once translated, your original profile remains unchanged, but members can now choose to search for your profile using their native language. You can also tweak how information appears in your translated profile to adjust how education, professional experience or other information appears in the second language.

10. **Include recommendations.** LinkedIn requires three recommendations for your profile to be considered "complete". However, many LinkedIn users shy away from asking for recommendations. LinkedIn recommendations have been the subject of significant debate for several years. Yes, these recommendations will never be 100% objective. Because LinkedIn is a public platform, no one is going to write a negative recommendation. (And clearly, a user would never choose to display a negative recommendation either.) When reading recommendations, it's important to apply filters: who wrote the recommendation? What was their relationship? Do the qualities in the recommendation match the user's profile? Social networks like LinkedIn succeed based on transparency and reputation. In this reputation economy, a recommendation from a well-connected and respected contact who has direct knowledge of your work adds credibility to your profile. Ask your boss, a coworker or former colleague for a

recommendation – and offer to write one back in return.

Chapter 6: Growing Your Network

The more contacts you have, the more powerful LinkedIn can be. Unlike Facebook, where some users may wish to be more exclusive with their friend lists, LinkedIn is a network where users will want to connect with (nearly) everyone they know professionally. However, just like in the offline professional world, LinkedIn connections are governed by business etiquette. Mastering LinkedIn connection etiquette will help you successfully grow your network without alienating potential contacts or having your LinkedIn account frozen.

Connection Etiquette on LinkedIn

On Twitter, anyone can follow anyone else – no one has to "confirm" a follower. On Facebook, anyone can request anyone else to be a friend – although the friend must confirm your friendship. On LinkedIn, however, you must have a pre-existing relationship with someone before you can connect. You will need to work together, belong to the same group, have worked at the same company, or attended the same school in order to connect. If you do not already have a clear connection, you will need to supply that person's email address in order to send a connection request. This is designed to cut down on spam and ensure that LinkedIn networks bring value to everyone.

As a professional network, LinkedIn is governed by business etiquette and courtesy as outlined in LinkedIn's user agreement. As a general rule of thumb, only ask to connect with people you actually know. If you send a request to someone who does not want to connect with you or does not know who you are, they can reject the request by selecting the "I don't know" option. This hurts your standing with LinkedIn. If too many people select the "I don't know" option, your account with be flagged for review and temporarily disabled.

If you'd like to get in touch with someone who you don't know directly, you can request an introduction from a primary contact. You can also develop a relationship with this person and then request a connection (see #3 in our list below).

Open vs. Selective Connectors

Is it ever okay to send a contact request to someone you don't know? Yes – if that person is an "open connector." Open connectors are open to invitations from anyone, even if you do not directly know them. Many open connectors will list "LION" in their profile title – this stands for "LinkedIn Open Networker". LIONs are open to networking with just about any business professionals, and thanks to the presence of LIONs on LinkedIn, disparate groups are linked together. This helps prevent the existence of large, closed groups and makes LinkedIn a more "linked in" place. Want to connect with a LION? You can search for LIONs in your career field or area of expertise by performing an advanced search and including "LION" in the search terms. Keep in mind, however, that simply because a user has "LION" in their title does not mean that they will accept your connection request. While they should (based on how they are advertising themselves), if a LION denies your request with an "I don't know", you'll be the one that's penalized.

10 Tips for Growing Your LinkedIn Network

In "Customizing LinkedIn", we discussed a few basic ways to expand your network. These include importing existing contact lists, exploring LinkedIn's "People You May Know" contact recommendations, and joining alumni groups. After you execute these basic growth strategies, don't wait passively for individuals to find you. Here are 10 additional ways to actively grow your LinkedIn network:

1. **Join an "Invites Welcome" group.** In addition to alumni and professional groups, there are many groups on LinkedIn dedicated exclusively to open networking. These groups are setup to connect open networkers with each other. Get started with the following three LION groups: "Lion500.com", "Windmill Networking", and "MyLink500". As a member of these groups, you'll have easy access to large, open networks with contacts who will be open to joining yours.

2. **Send a personalized invite.** The default invite, "I'd like to add you to my professional network" can come off as cold and impersonal. As a professional courtesy, take the time to add a personal line or two. Did you work with this person in the past? Do you have mutual contacts? Reference your work together and your respect/mutual appreciation for his/her professional accomplishments.

3. **Develop a relationship.** If you would like to connect with someone who does not directly

know you, initiate contact by building a relationship with them on LinkedIn. Start by answering one of their questions, joining a LinkedIn group to which they also belong, or sending them a LinkedIn "InMail" message (just be sure the message is relevant to a shared business interest or expertise). If you are a member of the same group, you can by-pass InMail and send a direct message.

4. **Check contact settings and profile.** Like any social network, there are plenty of LinkedIn users who signed up for a profile and simply forgot about it or infrequently check it. Other users will indicate in their contact settings that they are not interested in connecting with new people. After performing an advanced search for new contacts, check these settings carefully. Does their profile indicate that they are active on LinkedIn? In general, the more active individuals are on LinkedIn, the more open they will be to connecting with new or previously unknown contacts.

5. **Request an introduction.** Leverage the power of your network – request an introduction from a shared contact. Introductions are free to all users and allow you to contact someone who is two or three degrees away from you. To request an introduction, locate the user with whom you wish to be introduced. From their profile, click "Get introduced through a connection".

Chose from a list of possible people to make an introduction. Next, write a message to the person who would be introducing you clearly explaining why you would like the introduction.

6. **Send an InMail message.** Known as the "Hail Mary" of LinkedIn, InMail is a paid service that allows you to contact other users, even if you do not have an existing connection or relationship. InMail is included in paid memberships. If you don't have a paid membership, you can purchase the service a la carte; $10 purchases 10 message credits. LinkedIn bills InMail as a personalized form of email. Instead of a cold call or a random email, InMail includes professional information about you. LinkedIn claims this personal information "gives your recipient the confidence to respond." If you don't receive a reply to your message within seven days, LinkedIn lets you send another InMail message to another user for free.

7. **Reconnect with old friends.** On LinkedIn, it's easy to connect with colleagues and former colleagues – while forgetting about older friends and acquaintances, especially if they don't appear in your immediate professional or alumni circles. This is just one reason why importing contacts from Google or Outlook is so important. Even if you and your best friend from high school have never

worked together (and likely never will), becoming friends on LinkedIn will dramatically expand your contact circles.

8. **Give away your knowledge.** Participate in a LinkedIn forum and provide meaningful answers that really help people solve their problems. Sharing your knowledge demonstrates to others why you are such a valuable contact, and will naturally help grow you connections.

9. **Bring your existing social media contacts back to LinkedIn.** LinkedIn offers users a free LinkedIn connection badge. Do you have a personal website or blog? Then add this badge to your blog to encourage subscribers to connect with you. Do you have hundreds (or thousands) of Twitter followers? Tweet a message about your new LinkedIn profile and invite users to connect with you there.

10. **Be active in your LinkedIn groups.** Many LinkedIn groups have hundreds or thousands of members. While joining groups is crucial to building your network, simply adding your name to a long list of others brings you little benefit. Get active in group discussions. Post thoughtful questions and contribute helpful answers. Once you start making a name for yourself within the group, then you can feel confident asking group members to connect with you.

Chapter 7: Finding Jobs

LinkedIn has transformed the job search process, especially for individuals with advanced degrees seeking middle to upper level employment positions within companies. According to a 2011 study published by Education Advisory Board, 86.6 percent of human resource and recruiting specialists use LinkedIn. A 2012 article published by *U.S. News and World Report* also highlighted the overwhelming trend towards LinkedIn job searches. According to the report, business schools strongly advise MBA students to be active on LinkedIn, connecting with school alumni at targeted companies to arrange an informational interview. Joining school alumni organizations on LinkedIn are one way to stay active in networking discussion groups. But you don't need an MBA to make LinkedIn work for you. Here's what to do:

Using LinkedIn to Job Search While Unemployed

In an ideal world, no one would leave a job without having another one lined up. Thanks to the recent recession, however, thousands of LinkedIn job searchers are also currently unemployed. If this description matches your situation, be sure to update your profile to show that you are no longer at your old company. Are you doing freelance work on the side? Part-time consulting? It's never a good idea to mislead others regarding your current state of employment – only include this information if it's accurate.

It's also never good to sound desperate for work. Studies routinely show that companies prefer the passive job seeker to the active job seeker. A title that includes "Available for Immediate Hire" or "Actively Seeking Work" is one small step above "Will Work for Food" in the minds of many HR departments. Even if you are actively searching for your job, edit your headline to reflect that you are open to new opportunities while maintaining a level of professionalism. For example, a headline such as "Experienced Risk Management Executive Seeking My Next Great Opportunity" succinctly summarizes your previous experience while clarifying that you are actively job searching.

Use the summary area as an opportunity to clarify your situation. A title like "Interim Consultant Seeking New Position" lets others know that while you may not be fully employed, you aren't channel surfing all day either. Next, in the summary area, include a brief line about your current consulting work and then describe the new position that you seek. Are you looking for challenging work in human capital management? Then say so. This is especially important if you hope to transition from one field to another. Adding a brief description (including keywords) about a new target job will help your profile get noticed by the right people.

Using LinkedIn to Job Search While Employed

Job searching while employed is a delicate process. If your are connected to your current coworkers on LinkedIn, but they don't know about your job search, the last thing you want is for them to be blinded sided by a giant "job seeker" badge plastered to your profile. At the same time, you'll need to make it clear in your profile that you are searching for new opportunities. Follow these 10 tips to covertly job search while employed:

1. **Update your profile.** The first step of any LinkedIn job search is to ensure that your profile is 100% complete. Your summary is

the perfect place to highlight your accomplishments and indicate that you are open to new challenges and opportunities. According to LinkedIn, users with complete profiles are 40 times more likely to be contacted for opportunities. Don't let missing information hold you back. A simple "open to new, challenging opportunities in XXX field" indicates that you are interested and available without sounding desperate – or alarming co-workers that you're about to jump ship. If you are re-writing your profile, do so in a word document first. This is an easy way to catch spelling and grammar errors, and it makes optimization for keywords fast and easy.

2. **Update your network.** Does your network reflect your real world connections? In the rush to grow your network as large as possible, it's easy to overlook the real world connections that matter most. Are you connected with a former boss or coworker who can give you a recommendation or job introduction? If you've let your LinkedIn network stagnate, now is the time to actively review and grow it to include your most trusted connections.

3. **Message key network contacts**. If your job search isn't public knowledge, reach out to key network contacts. Let them know that you are looking and identify which fields/jobs you are interested in. This is especially important

for contacts at companies where you might like to work. Ask for an informational interview to learn more about their position and company.

4. **Research recruiters and interviewers**. No one enters an interview without background knowledge on the company or interviewer. Don't just do a simple Google search – use LinkedIn to find out in-depth information about the interviewer, including past job positions and alumni memberships. LinkedIn is an easy way to find out if you have common connections, which may give you an edge over other interviewees. You can then steer your conversation to naturally bring up these mutual connections. It should go without saying, but an overt "I saw on LinkedIn that you know my old college roommate" is a bit too much for an initial interview; naturally guide the conversation in that direction.

5. **Download the jobs insider toolbar**. This toolbar integrates with your web browser, so when you are viewing a company's external website, you can see what connections you have inside the company. Leverage these connections to boost your chance of landing an informational interview or standing out to recruiters.

6. **Add recommendations**. Yes, recommendations are subjective. But they add

credibility and transparency to your profile, especially when they come from trusted sources that have a connection to your dream company or job. If you don't have any recommendations, ask a former co-worker, boss or colleague for one – and offer to give one back in return. There's a good chance these are the same folks who will also serve as references, so asking for a LinkedIn recommendation is a great way to break the ice.

7. **Make your profile public**. This seems basic, but surprisingly many LinkedIn users keep their profiles private and prevent them from showing up in search results. If you're searching for a job, a private profile does you no good. Be sure that you also have a custom URL link.

8. **Add skills to your profile**. If you've been a LinkedIn member since its early days, then you may have missed the addition of "skills" to the profile. This area allows users to add publications, languages, certifications and patents. LinkedIn's 2011 IPO showed that 40% of the company's revenue came from their "Hiring Solutions" software. It's a safe assumption that the skills, publications, languages, certifications and patents fields correspond with the same specialty fields that HR departments use to find the perfect

candidate.

9. **Add LinkedIn applications**. Applications allow you to add additional, insightful information to your profile. For example, if you are a new media consultant and have a personal blog dedicated to your SEO and social media tips, add an app that links your blog feed directly to your profile.

10. **Research and follow companies**. LinkedIn users now have the ability to follow companies, which allows you to hear about new job opportunities, hires and departures first. Company search allows you to search for companies by location, industry and size, as well as shared connections. Your results will be personalized by keywords and search filters. Company search is a great way to get started identifying potential employers. Following companies keeps you in the loop.

Using LinkedIn "Jobs You May Be Interested In"

LinkedIn's "Jobs for You" has thousands of job postings that can be searched by keywords, company, location and title. The "Jobs you may be interested in" is a beta service that shows a list of jobs specifically targeted to job candidates. Based on your keywords and experience profile, LinkedIn selects several jobs to list on your home page. This is ideal for both active and passive seekers because the jobs are sitting right there waiting for you to learn more, if you so desire. No searching required. You can access LinkedIn's "Jobs you may be interested in" by going to Jobs -> Find Jobs.

Paid Job Seeker Accounts

LinkedIn offers job seekers three levels of paid account service. All levels include access to the "job seeker community", a webinar on "job seeking on LinkedIn", placement at the top of lists as a "featured applicant", detailed salary information to target six-figure jobs, and a full list of everyone who has viewed your profile.

- **Job Seeker Basic** ($19.95/mo) – 10 introductions to targeted companies, does not include InMail
- **Job Seeker** ($29.95/mo) – 15 introductions to targeted companies, five InMails per month ($50 value)

- **Job Seeker Plus** ($49.95/mo) – 25 introductions to targeted companies, 10 InMails per month ($100 value)

Should you upgrade to a paid job seeker account?
If you plan to send a lot of InMails each month, it makes financial sense to have a paid job seeker account. You'll enjoy added benefits, like detailed salary information and placement at the top of lists as a "featured applicant", while saving money on the overall cost of InMails. For this reason, we recommend trying Job Seeker ($29.95) for one month. During this month, are you able to take advantage of LinkedIn's enhanced job search capabilities? Do the InMails you send help advance your job search? The majority of job applicants on LinkedIn find their jobs through primary or secondary contacts, rather than InMail or searching job forums. However, the majority of job seekers also do not sign up for a paid account. A trial month of Job Seeker is a good way to determine whether this account makes sense for your job searching needs.

Chapter 8: Recruiting Job Candidates

Have you ever Googled a candidate prior to a job interview? What about looking a candidate up on Facebook or Twitter? In all likelihood, you've done a little Google research before bringing a candidate in for an interview. While LinkedIn won't uncover college frat party photos, looking a candidate up on the networking service is the fastest way to get a quick snapshot of their professional interests, accomplishments, and academic background. But LinkedIn is useful for far more than just a quick professional background check – it's an invaluable resource for identifying and recruiting potential job candidates.

Using LinkedIn to Find Job Candidates

When you need a specific candidate, the last thing you want to do is post your job opening on Monster.com, CareerBuilder.com or Craigslist. Your human resource department will be spammed with hundreds of resumes from unqualified applicants desperate for a job. Worse, the most qualified applicants may not even be actively job searching, and miss your posting all together. Your best bet is to use your LinkedIn network for job recruitment. There are over 130,000 recruiters on LinkedIn. If you don't actively recruit on LinkedIn, you'll miss out on the chance to reach out to qualified applicants first.

Five Tips for Recruiting Job Candidates on LinkedIn

1. **Search for employees based on a current or past employer.** Do several companies employ people with skills similar to those that your company needs? Search for past and present employees of these companies. You can also search based on recommendations from trusted connections.

2. **Keyword search for 'new opportunities' or 'new challenges'.** Many individuals who are open to new job options will add a line that includes "Seeking My Next Great Opportunity" or "Open to New Challenges". Searching for these terms reinforces

LinkedIn's existence as a "find and be found network" – you'll be searching through profiles of individuals who have identified a desire to seek "new opportunities" or "new challenges" within a specific field – and that's exactly what your business will be offering.

3. **Expand your network.** Raise your profile by joining groups and participating in LinkedIn's "Answers" section. These are two easy ways to expand your network and reach new potential recruits. When selecting groups, pick a topic or purpose that goes beyond the reach of your company's brand. For example, if you provide human resource software, you might choose a more general group on software development or human resource management. A broader group opens you up to a greater number of people that are tangentially qualified for your company. Their present jobs may not be identical to the one you have open, but you can be confident that their skill sets and interests will be relevant.

4. **Send InMail.** Once you've identified potential candidates, send an InMail message to begin a conversation. LinkedIn guarantees a response with InMail, so if you target does not reply, you'll be able to message another prospective job candidate free of charge.

5. **Post new opportunities in the Career tab on your company page.** Advertise new

opportunities with a posting on the career tab of your company page. Your company page will also contain additional information about your business' brand and links to application forms, making it easy for potential recruits to apply. While this is a passive recruiting strategy, it lets job seekers know that you are hiring, giving candidates you might otherwise have missed the opportunity to apply.

Using LinkedIn "Jobs for You" Ads

LinkedIn "Jobs for You" ads is a paid service that delivers personalized job recommendations to passive job candidates, posting highly targeted web-wide ads. The service allows you to reach candidates wherever they browse, targeting candidates by professional background. Based on profile data, LinkedIn uses an algorithm to ensure the ads are visible to relevant candidates, even if they're just checking the local weather forecast. "Jobs for You" ads can be expensive, however, and as a recruiting solution, these ads are best geared towards major corporations. Smaller businesses will have greater success with the five tips discussed above.

Paid Recruiter Membership: Do I Need One?

If a preliminary search did not turn up any qualified candidates, or you've been unsuccessful in your attempts to find candidates that match your needs, consider upgrading to a paid account. LinkedIn offers accounts specifically for recruiters, such as the "Talent Finder" account ($99.95/mo), which includes 25 InMails per month (a $250 value), premium and talent filters, 700 search results, group search access and profile organizer. Premium and talent filters allow for expanded search capabilities beyond a normal advanced search. Premium filters search fields for seniority, company size, interests and Fortune 1000. Talent filters include years of experience, function, groups and whether a user is new to LinkedIn. Members with free accounts receive only 100 profile results when they perform a search – even if hundreds more match their criteria. With a paid talent account, you'll have access to up to 10 times as many search results. A paid account is also valuable for time management. LinkedIn will automatically run saved searches and send an email alert when a candidate matches specific search criteria, so you can spend less time searching and more time connecting with job candidates.

Job Recruitment Case Study: Accenture

In 2011, Accenture won the "Social Marketing: LinkedIn" award from *BtoB Magazine* for the company's job recruitment strategy targeting LinkedIn subgroups. While Accenture's careers group has more than 5,000 members, its real strength lies in its extensive subgroups. A different Accenture consultant manages each subgroup. Direct management of the subgroups, which are organized by professional specialty and geography, ensure prompt and complete answers to any member questions. By building a strong relationship with potential hires, Accenture successfully leverages LinkedIn's networks to identify, target and recruit the strongest job candidates. As of the 2011 Social Marketing awards, Accenture's LinkedIn campaign had already generated several strong company hires that might otherwise have not been possible without LinkedIn recruitment. According to *BtoB Magazine*, "Those (new hire) numbers are likely to grow significantly as word-of-mouth spreads. Accenture has laid the foundation for a new and much more effective approach to recruitment."

Chapter 9: Using LinkedIn in Business

Company Pages & Sales Leads

LinkedIn Company Pages

LinkedIn company pages exist to allow job seekers and professionals to conduct research on a specific company. Users can search for company pages by keyword, location, industry, Fortune status, company size and number of followers. Companies may manage the following pages:

- **Overview page:** Shows who connects a user to the company, information on employers, Twitter updates, recent blog posts, news articles and statistics
- **Statistics page:** User generated content provides information for potential job seekers, including a summary of current employees (work experience, educational degrees, positions) and business intelligence data for sales and development opportunities (former employees, recommended employees, etc.)

- **Careers page:** Current job openings
- **Products & Services page:** Created by the company to showcase its products and services; LinkedIn users can recommend specific products or services here.

Users who click the "follow company" button will receive updates from the company on new job openings, new hires, and employee departures. Users will also receive updates in their newsfeed.

LinkedIn Company Page vs. Facebook Fan Page: What's the Difference?

A good way to understand a LinkedIn company page is to compare it to a Facebook Fan Page. Facebook Fan Pages exist for individuals to "like" a page and receive information in their newsfeed from the company. These pages exist to build viral marketing campaigns about new products and services by generating social media buzz. Companies may also launch special applications, run giveaways and other contests through their pages. In contrast, a company page is about connecting with potential employees and clients. While branding your company is important, there are not giveaways or viral videos. In comparison to Facebook, the audience visiting a LinkedIn fan page is older, more mature and visiting for professional purposes.

Five Tips for Creating a LinkedIn Company Page

1. **Take control.** Many companies are surprised to learn that a company page already exists. This is because LinkedIn automatically creates pages based on a user's professional information. The first step to improving your company's page is taking control. Start by defining who the administrators of your page will be. LinkedIn allows anyone with a registered email address that matches your company's domain to become an

administrator. However, since there is virtually no social engagement on a LinkedIn page (it simply provides information), there's no need to for a high number of page admins. Designate one or two users who will be responsible for posting status updates.

2. **Build your brand.** Start by uploading a logo for the general company page. You can also upload an alternate square logo, which will appear when status updates are posted. This logo is essential since it will become the visual "face" of your company to LinkedIn. If your current logo does not easily fit into a square, have a graphic designer spend a few minutes tweaking your logo to ensure the dimensions and resolution are correct.

3. **Optimize for keywords.** Just like a user profile, your company profile can also be optimized for keywords. Enter a brief company description and then include company specialties. For example, if you are a social media consulting firm, your profile might list "social media training", "social media ROI", and "Facebook consulting".

4. **Include location.** Do you provide an offline product or service? If you work remotely as a consultant, location is not as important. But if you provide a localized service or product, location is paramount. Be sure that you can be found in search results by including your

company address and zip code.

5. **Be social.** Companies can now publish status updates for their followers, sharing relevant industry news and company announcements. In April 2012, LinkedIn introduced a new feature called "Targeted Company Updates". This allows companies to deliver relevant content to the right audience. This increases followers engagement and loyalty to a specific business brand. It also has important applications for candidate recruitment. To target information to a specific audience, any company administrator may click the "Share with" dropdown menu and select "Targeted Audience" (the default is "All Followers"). You can choose to include your current company employees or only message non-employees. Next, you can choose between company size, industry, function (e.g. research, accounting, administrative), seniority, type of employee (e.g., senior, manager, VP), or geography. Followers who match these criteria will see the company update on their homepage. For example, your company can use this to announce a job opening to potential job candidates in a specific industry.

Using LinkedIn to Generate Sales Leads

LinkedIn is a unique opportunity to actually network with fellow companies in pursuit of jobs, capital investments, project coordination and sales leads. Just like job searching and candidate recruitment, sales lead generation starts with a strong network. Employees at your company that are responsible for sales should join industry groups and participate in forums, providing free expert advice. As a company, focus on growing your LinkedIn company page membership. Companies may also wish to sign up for a paid LinkedIn account, such as the "Sales Navigator" account ($49.95/mo), which includes 10 InMails per month (a $100 value), Lead Builder, premium search filters, access to a full list of people who view your profile and 25 Profile Organizer folders for contact organization. Lead Builder is an especially useful feature; it allows users to create and save lists of prospects, which can be organized with Profile Organizer.

When using LinkedIn for prospecting and sales lead generation, remember that LinkedIn is a networking service first, not a marketplace. Users that push a hard sell may have their memberships revoked if other users complain. Any hard sells should take place outside LinkedIn; this will protect your professional reputation on the network and your account's integrity.

Sales Leads Case Study: Ultimate Software

Ultimate Software, which makes human capital management solutions, launched a multi-pronged LinkedIn campaign to generate sales leads and new customers. When the campaign began, Ultimate Software's LinkedIn page received little traffic. The company used social media business cards, conference promotions and an online contest to drive traffic to its LinkedIn group. Company experts regularly joined group discussions, providing free, expert advice in response to member questions. Thanks to increased visibility and engagement, group membership rose by 236% in one year, with many members posting referrals to encourage their network contacts to join the community. The LinkedIn group referred more than 6,100 unique visitors to the company website, which in turn led to 107 sales leads and six deals. Ultimate Software also won the 2012 "Social Marketing: LinkedIn" award from *BtoB Magazine*.

Chapter 10: Using LinkedIn Answers

LinkedIn Answers is a service that allows LinkedIn members to post questions to the LinkedIn community and receive fast, accurate answers from experts. This is also an ideal opportunity to showcase your knowledge with expertise solutions, which helps build your LinkedIn reputation. Participating in LinkedIn Answers either as a questioner or a respondent helps you stay up-to-date on the latest in your industry.

Asking a Question

Specific questions allow LinkedIn members to showcase their knowledge, experience or opinions. Asking a question is a great way to receive expert information for free.

1. To ask your question, select the "More" option from the top menu bar and choose "Answers".
2. Select "Ask a question" from the Answers sub-menu.

3. Enter your question; to help the right members find it, be sure to categorize your question and add specifics.
4. Your question will be posted to the LinkedIn Answers Home page; your contacts will also see that you've asked a question.
5. To check responses to your current or past questions, go to "My Q&A".
6. After people post answers, you can choose with person answered your question the best.

Prior to asking your question, you may wish to conduct an "Advanced Answers Search" to ensure that your question has not already been answered before. This search feature is also useful if you are not satisfied with the answers that you receive to your question – it may have been answered better in the past.

NOTE: Do not ask a question that specifically promotes your company's product or service, announces your job search or seeks to recruit candidates for your company. These questions will be flagged and removed. Prior to posting your question, LinkedIn will ask if it is related to recruiting, promoting or job seeking. If so, you will need to categorize it as such. LinkedIn will also recommend other means for asking your question, such as posting your job on LinkedIn or using LinkedIn's job search.

Answering a Question

To answer a question, go to the Answers Home page. You can see a continually updated feed with the latest questions. You can also search for questions in different categories, ranging from "Using LinkedIn" to "Sustainability."

To earn an expertise rating on LinkedIn, find questions in the areas that you know by browsing familiar categories. Post public answers to the questions; while you can keep your answer private (and only share with the questioner), doing so won't help you earn expertise. Every time that a questioner selects your answer as "the best", you will earn one expertise point. The more points of expertise you earn, the higher your name will appear on an "experts list". You will also be highlighted on the Answers home page as a "Top Expert" for the week.

Remember, people post questions because they genuinely need help. This is not the place to make a hard sell or a sales pitch. Win potential clients over with your free, expert knowledge. Any spamming, job recruitment or sales pitches will be flagged for violating LinkedIn's user terms – and you may find that your account is revoked.

Chapter 11: Go Mobile - LinkedIn on Mobile Phones & CardMuch

LinkedIn Mobile App

Take your network with you! LinkedIn offers free mobile apps for Blackberry, iPhone and Palm Pre. While not specifically designed for the iPad, the iPhone app still works great on this platform. The app features a home screen with updates and LinkedIn today news articles, similar to the web-based home. The app will also suggest industries and news to follow based on your connections, or you can search for other industries.

The LinkedIn app is meeting-centric and perfect for quickly researching someone while rushing to meet them. Users can pull up background information while on the go, which is ideal if you need more information about a potential job candidate or client and are already on your way to meet them. You can also quickly scan the news articles to find the latest news in your industry (or your potential client's industry) in order to sound informed prior to the meeting. After the meeting, it's easy to connect with your client, or permanently disconnect, as the case may be. The mobile app is also ideal for tradeshows or major conferences. No longer will you have a giant stack of business cards to sort through (or sit forgotten in the back of your desk drawer) – now, you can instantly connect with contacts right after meeting them.

CardMuch

Ready to say goodbye to business cards permanently? Then LinkedIn's newly launched CardMuch app is for you. Tech Crunch named "CardMuch" one of its "Top 20 Apps" for iPhone 4S, and after just using it once, it's easy to see why. Millions of business cards are exchanged each day. The CardMuch app allows you to capture a digital image of a business card, add it to your contact list, and connect to that person's profile. Once a card is scanned, this information is mapped to your contact's LinkedIn profile. Not only will you know a person's name, title, employer and basic contact info, but you'll also have full access to their LinkedIn profile, including past employers, education and contacts. And you won't need to spend time sifting through a rolodex – your contacts are with you wherever you go.

Conclusion

While many people use LinkedIn primarily to search for new jobs, this professional network can be useful for many different reasons. For example, LinkedIn can help journalists establish a personal brand, gather background information about a potential interviewee, connect with new story sources and come up with fresh story ideas. Do you own a small business? LinkedIn is an easy way to let contacts know about your company, build your business' brand through referrals and recommendations, and even find new employees when your business begins to grow. Need help recruiting job candidates? LinkedIn's paid recruitment services can help you target and identify specific candidates.

To learn more tips for customizing LinkedIn to your specific needs, be sure to check out LinkedIn's "User Guides" in the LinkedIn Learning Center. These guides include specific information for small businesses, students, job seekers, entrepreneurs, journalists, nonprofit groups, and more.

About Minute Help Press

Minute Help Press is building a library of books for people with only minutes to spare. Follow @minutehelp on Twitter to receive the latest information about free and paid publications from Minute Help Press, or visit minutehelp.com.

Cover Image © Photosani - Fotolia.com

2184576R00038

Printed in Great Britain
by Amazon.co.uk, Ltd.,
Marston Gate.